Janet

WHEN SORROW COMES

WHEN SORROW COMES

Robert V. Ozment

Fleming H. Revell Company
Old Tappan, New Jersey

All Scripture quotations, except otherwise noted, are from the Revised Standard Version of the Bible copyright 1946 and 1952 by the Division of Christian Education of the National Council of the Churches of Christ in the United States of America, and are used by permission.

Scripture quotation identified KJV is from the King James Version of the Bible.

Grateful acknowledgment is made to the following for permission to reprint copyright material: Mrs. Helen Armstrong Straub for the poem "Resigned" by Dorothy Dix Porges; Coslett Publishing Company, Williamsport, Pennsylvania, for the poem "Vespers" by Silas Weir Mitchell; Evangelical Publishers, Toronto, Canada, for the poem "For Thou Art With Me" by Annie Johnson Flint, from *The Best Loved Poems of Annie Johnson Flint*. Reproduced by permission. Appreciation is expressed also to the Houghton Mifflin Company for the use of two stanzas from the poem "The Eternal Goodness" by John Greenleaf Whittier, and to Harper and Row, Publishers, for the poems on pages 66, 69, 78, 79, and 82, reprinted from *Masterpieces of Religious Verse*.

Library of Congress Catalog Card Number: 78-111964

ISBN 0-8007-1633-7

All rights reserved. No part of this publication may be reproduced, stored in a retrieval system, or transmitted in any form or by any means—electronic, mechanical, photocopy, recording or any other—except for brief quotations in printed reviews, without the prior permission of the publisher.

Copyright © 1970 by Word Books,
1989 rights reverted to Robert Ozment,
©1989 by Robert V. Ozment
Published by the Fleming H. Revell Company
Old Tappan, New Jersey 07675
Printed in the United States of America

ACKNOWLEDGMENT

The author wishes to express his deep gratitude to his secretary, Mrs. Verne M. Bennett, for her invaluable help in securing permissions for copyright material used in this book, and for her careful typing of the manuscript.

To my friend,
the late Sandy B. Lewis, whose generous
and brief thirty-nine years on earth
brought immeasurable joy to many
who never knew him

CONTENTS

Foreword.	9
WHEN SORROW COMES	15
DEATH IS GOD'S PLAN	25
WAS IT THE WILL OF GOD?	29
MAGIC LIGHT OF FAITH	32
WHAT IS HEAVEN LIKE?	35
THROUGH THE VALLEY	38
WHAT TO DO	41
THERE IS A FUTURE	51
NO LAST TIME!	55
INSPIRATIONAL POEMS	63
COMFORTING SCRIPTURE	85
PRAYER	95

FOREWORD

Some books die before they are ever born. They never find a place on a bookstore shelf. Other books live a short, anemic life and soon take their places among forgotten things. Still other books, and they are few, deal with what an ancient writer called "the universal need," and so not only survive, but stand tall against the tide that flows in an endless stream from the printing presses of the world. Dr. Robert Ozment, pastor of Atlanta's First Methodist Church, has written such a book.

When Sorrow Comes is small in size but encompasses a need in every life—either now, or later. If you live long enough, you will lose someone you love. If your life is shortened, then someone will lose you. In either case, a broken heart will reach out through the dark, searching for a hand to hold, for a word that will turn weakness into strength.

There is no exception.

. . . .

Whether the Cup with sweet or bitter run,
The Wine of Life keeps ebbing drop by drop,
The Leaves of Life keep falling one by one.

—*The Rubáiyát of Omar Khayyám*

The chapter entitled "What Is Heaven Like?" is one of the shortest in the book—and justly so. We know very little about the nature of heaven, but what we do know is sufficient for our needs. Although each of us has his own ideas about what heaven is like, we can all find in the promise, "Where I am, there shall ye be also," ample reassurance.

Perhaps the most turned-to part of the book will be the inspirational poems and comforting quotations. They should probably be read when we "sit alone with life" and consider its great problems. In these poems and quotations may be found the answer to many of the questions about which we ponder.

If you are among that endless throng that has "loved and lost," I recommend this book. If you have, so far, escaped passage along that lonely road, then I recommend that you place the book on your library shelf—you will need it one of these days.

PIERCE HARRIS
Pastor Emeritus

First Methodist Church
Atlanta, Georgia

WHEN SORROW COMES

WHEN SORROW COMES

"TELL ME about death," the little girl asked her father.

"Death," he began, "is God's plan for us. It's like the way that, after you have played all day and night comes, you often fall asleep in my big chair. I take you in my arms and place you in your bed. The next morning when you awake, you are in the room we planned and prepared for you. Death is like that," he said.

I want to tell you about death. But when you write about death, you also write about life. The two cannot be separated.

When you lose a loved one, you are hurt. The grief of separation is not easy to overcome, but it can be done. I want to tell you how.

God can and will lead you safely through the

valley of sorrow, if you will let **Him**. As inevitably as the darkness of night is followed by the morning light and the dreariness of winter by the awakening promise of spring, so too in time your feeling of grief will yield to the realization that your loved one is continuing to grow spiritually in eternal life. You need God now. You have always needed Him, but now especially you must have His strength and help to sustain you in the difficult walk through the shadows of loneliness.

Many people do not like to think or talk about death. Perhaps this is because we do not understand death. It frequently comes like a thief in the night to rob us of one we love dearly. It leaves us with shattered hopes, crushed dreams, and a gnawing emptiness which is almost indescribable.

For many years, in our culture, we have attempted to obscure the reality of death. Every effort is made to have the body appear lifelike when it is placed in the casket. We cover the casket with beautiful flowers and spread artificial grass around the grave. Yet the heart aches with a pain so deep that it seems to be almost beyond comfort.

Before we can see death in the proper light,

we must first see life in its true perspective. God is the Creator of both the universe and life. Keep in mind that He did not make us to live on earth forever. Jesus said to His disciples, "I go to the Father" (John 16:16). Our bodies wear out, and this earthly environment is not suited for us to continue in it forever. Some of us stay here a very short time, while others remain for several decades. But life on earth is just one phase of our existence.

Although we love the earth, God has something better for His children. Our Lord said, "In my Father's house are many rooms; if it were not so, would I have told you that I go to prepare a place for you? And when I go and prepare a place for you, I will come again and will take you to myself, that where I am you may be also" (John 14:2-3).

Jesus was saying two things here. First, He was telling us that at the end of this earthly pilgrimage we do not drop off into oblivion and a sea of nothingness. Death is not the end of life. And, secondly, He was revealing to us the fact that God has made adequate provisions for us. He has prepared a place where there are many mansions. He implies that in heaven all shall be together as members of God's family.

Did you ever consider the orderliness of our existence? All of us enter the physical world through the door of birth. Yet, we know that human life does not begin at the moment of birth. Actually, we are approximately nine months old when we make our first appearance. The miraculous process of life begins at the moment of conception.

Eventually we must die. Death is the door that leads from this life to the next. Those who believe in the Christian faith know that death is not the end of human existence any more than the experience of birth was the beginning. Death, then, is in many ways like birth. Birth ushers the infant into a larger world of beauty, color, sense, sound, and unlimited possibilities of growth. The Christian view of death is quite similar. The experience of death brings us to another world abundant in spiritual truths and adventure. It is a larger world of beauty and love and possibilities that stretch beyond our fondest dreams. I like to think of death as expressed in these lines:

As I walk through the darkness to morning light
   The rays of dawn follow every night;
I take a step by faith and see
   The footprints of God in front of me.

Though the path of life be a strange one for us, it is familiar to God.

When John Quincy Adams was eighty years old, a friend inquired, "How is John Quincy Adams today?"

"Quite well, I thank you," replied the former president, "but the house in which he lives is becoming dilapidated; in fact, almost uninhabitable. I think John Quincy Adams will have to move out before long. But he, himself, is well, quite well."

I was preaching a series of sermons in a church a few years ago when the tragic news reached a young woman who was attending these services, that her husband was dead. A plane had crashed, killing all aboard.

Added agony came to her because it was days before all the bodies could be identified. Yet she did not miss a service during the entire week. We all admired her serenity and self-composure during such a trying interval.

Before I left, I asked her to write me some of the thoughts she entertained during that difficult time. I wanted her to tell me, especially, what she found to sustain her.

It was some months before a letter came. I want to share with you a few of her thoughts.

"For the first few days," she wrote, "I lived with the question, 'Why, God?' Then, that question changed and I began asking 'Which way, God?' God never answered that first question, but He did answer the second one.

"The first thing that helped sustain me was a sense of gratitude. I was grateful for the years God gave my husband and me together. They were happy and wonderful years. At first, I felt cheated, but then I knew God had richly blessed us. We packed a lot of living into those fourteen years we were married. The golden memory of those years helped sustain me.

"Then, I knew life had to go on. My mother always taught us that as long as there was life, we had a responsibility to God and others. All of us are hurt on the journey through life, but it would be wrong to pull down the shades and shut the door.

"Finally, I was sustained by the presence of God. He was with me as I stumbled down the lonely road of sorrow. I have come through the dark night and felt the touch of His Hand."

When we lose a loved one, a sense of loneliness sweeps over us. We find it unthinkable to continue life. Part of this feeling, at least, arises because we are thinking only of ourselves. It is difficult, if not impossible, to visualize life without the one we have lost. Yet, the purpose of life is never centered, wholly, on a loved one. It is always centered on God. Thomas Carlyle, the Scottish essayist and historian, once said, "The older I grow—and I now stand on the brink of eternity—the more comes back to me that sentence in the Catechism I learned when a child, and the fuller its meaning becomes: 'What is the chief end of man? To glorify God and enjoy Him forever.' "

It is true that life will never be the same, because the circumstances will be different. Yet, life must go on. Our purpose and our destiny do not die with the one who is gone. We have certain responsibilities to God, to ourselves, and to others. Tomorrow can be faced with courage and the burdens we bear can be carried triumphantly.

Jesus taught that "with God all things are possible" (Matthew 19:26). He never sought to hide the risks we must assume in life. He emphasized the fact that trouble is a certainty: "In the world you have tribulation; but be of good cheer, I have overcome the world" (John 16:33). Again, He challenged those who wanted to be His disciples with the words, ". . . take up the cross, and follow me" (Mark 10:21, KJV). Nowhere are we taught that the journey through life will be easy, but everywhere we are assured that it will be possible. When the way is blurred and the future uncertain, just place your hand in God's hand and walk unafraid. He will never forsake you. The Gentle Galilean said, "... I am with you always ..." (Matthew 28:20). Joshua received an encouraging word from God when he succeeded Moses in leading the children of Israel to the Promised Land—"... I will be with you; I will not fail you or forsake you" (Joshua 1:5).

Life can often be wonderful. It can lift us to mountain peaks, where we march by the drums of joy. But then, it may thrust us into the dark and dingy valleys where we must walk by faith. Both the mountain peaks and the valleys have their place—joy and faith are both necessary.

Have you ever blamed God for the tragedies you don't understand? Many people have. When a man whose only son was killed recently in Vietnam received that sad news, his knees shook and his lips trembled. His first reaction was something like this: "Okay, God, why don't You come down from Your place in the sky and do something? Why do You let things like this happen? He was my only son." Bitterness filled his life, but finally one dark night he surrendered his grief to God. He had tried to live without God, but he had found life too difficult. He fell on his knees and prayed, "God forgive me and help me."

Then, he heard a Voice. "I know how you feel. My only Son died on the cross. I will help you." And even though that didn't change the hard facts, it did make life possible.

My good friend Ronald R. Meredith tells the story of waiting expectantly in a hospital during the birth of a son. Although the baby looked healthy enough when he arrived, the parents soon learned that he didn't have all the equipment sufficient to meet the rugged demands of life.

During that first year, Ron Meredith and his wife haunted the offices of specialists all over the country, trying to find the key which would unlock their son's mind. They never found it. But, they found something even greater. They found a faith that has been adequate for them and inspiring to others. Ron Meredith believes that God will never be satisfied until every life is complete. He wrote, "Someday, I'm going to look at Ronnie and say, 'Hi, Son,' and for the first time he will be able to smile intelligently, and answer, 'Hi, Dad.' We'll have so much to talk about," he continued, "for my Ronnie has never spoken a word."

DEATH IS GOD'S PLAN

DEATH IS A PART of God's plan for us, and while I do not understand it fully, I know it is both a good and wise plan. I wish each one of us could accept death with the same assurance and unwavering faith that our Lord accepted the cross. He did not want to go to Calvary, but at the age of thirty-three He found Himself struggling up that steep hill of suffering. Just as He knew God could be trusted and so committed His spirit into His Father's hands, let us also place our trust in Him when death comes to one we love.

Michelangelo Buonarroti, the Italian sculptor and painter, was discussing death with an old friend, near the end of his own life. His friend commented, "After such a good life, it is hard to look death in the eye." "Not at all!"

interrupted Michelangelo. "Since life was such a pleasure, death, coming from the same great source, cannot displease us."

During World War I, Sir Harry Lauder, the Scottish singer and comedian, received news that his son had been killed in France. His comment was, "In a time like this, there are three courses open to a man. He may give way to despair, sour upon the world and become a grouch. He may endeavor to drown his sorrow in drink, or by a life of waywardness and wickedness. Or, he may turn to God." Sir Harry Lauder turned to God and found the strength he needed.

When the clouds of sorrow begin to descend, one may be tempted to discard his faith and walk alone, but the wise person will turn to God for strength and help. Helen Keller wrote, "I, too, have loved and lost; I, too must often fight hard to keep a steadfast faith. When I fail to hear the Divine Voice, grief overwhelms me, my faith wavers; but I must not let it go, for without faith there would be no light in the world. Faith lifts up shining arms and points to a happier world where our loved ones await us."

J. H. Jowett reminds us that the range of

threescore and ten years is not the limit of our lives. We are not, like a lake, landlocked in the shoreline of seventy years; we are a part of the sea. "Death is not the end; it is only a beginning. Death is not the master of the house; he is only the porter at the King's lodge, appointed to open the gate and let the King's guests into the realm of eternal day. And so shall we ever be with the Lord."

Our faith in the goodness of God is undergirded in this statement about immortality by William Jennings Bryan: "If the Father deigns to touch, with Divine Power, the cold and pulseless heart of the buried acorn, and to make it burst from its prison walls, will He leave neglected in the earth . . . man, made in the image of his Creator? If he so stoops to give the rose bush, whose withered blossoms float upon the autumn breeze, the sweet assurance of another springtime, will He withhold the Words of Hope from the souls of men, when the frosts of winter come? If matter, mute and inanimate, though changed by the forces of nature into a multitude of forms, can never die, will the spirit of man suffer annihilation, when it has paid a brief visit like a royal guest, to this tenement of clay? No, I am as sure that there is another life as I am that I live today."

Archibald Rutledge, in his book *Children of Swamp and Wood*, expressed his faith in immortality with these words: "And when the time comes for our migration hence to a land unknown, through a misty darkness, He will not desert us. In the rainy night . . . the frailest abide secure. In that flight, amid other spheres than ours, I believe we shall know what it means to be sustained by Everlasting Arms.

"The migration of the birds ends in finding their desired haven. Shall we, then, doubt the end of our migration, when He goes with us all the way? 'I will never leave thee nor forsake thee.' "

WAS IT THE WILL OF GOD?

WE WERE JUST LEAVING the cemetery where we had left the body of a precious little girl. We walked together in silence. The father, a good Christian, broke the silence by saying, "I want to believe it is the will of God, but I can't."

Some people find comfort in attributing most everything that happens to the will of God. It is impossible for finite minds fully to understand God's will, or to see it clearly and completely in all the suffering and tragedy people endure.

Dr. Leslie Weatherhead, the English preacher, wrote a little book entitled *The Will of God,* in which he divides the will of God into three parts. First, he talks about God's "intentional will." By this he means what God actually intended to happen in your life and mine. It is obvious that God did not intend all the trouble and travail we see in life. Certainly, the God we see reflected in the life of Jesus did not intend for almost every generation of our finest men and women to march to bloody battlefields in order to preserve what we believe is good in our way of life. Man, with his free will, gets in the way of God's intentional will.

When God's intentional will is disturbed, what then? Weatherhead suggests that God has a "circumstantial will." God is not defeated just because His intentional will has been thwarted. He has a will for us in every set of circumstances.

Finally, Weatherhead talks about God's "ultimate will." By God's ultimate will we simply mean that the ultimate purposes of God may be hindered, but they can never be defeated. No matter what happens, trouble and tragedy can never finally defeat God. Don't forget, God has an eternity in which to achieve His ultimate will.

Death is the will of God. This is His plan, but the manner in which we meet death may not be God's will at all. Yet, His ultimate plan for the redemption of man cannot be defeated by all the evil that surrounds us. Evil speaks loud and long, but God speaks last. "I am the Alpha and the Omega, the first and the last, the beginning and the end" (Revelation 22:13). Even in death God has the final word, and that final word is "life."

MAGIC LIGHT OF FAITH

SOMETHING I have often said, and to many people, is that everyone needs a little magic light in order to see how to pass victoriously through some of the dark valleys. Faith is that magic light. Belief in God and trust in the teachings of Jesus will safely guide us through the dark valley of sorrow. MacDonald Clarke wrote, "Death, to a good man, is but passing through a dark entry, out of one little dusky room of his Father's house, into another that is fair and large, lightsome and glorious, and divinely entertaining."

The lines that follow express my idea of death.

The one I have loved is not lost—just gone;
   He's just moved from these shores of sand and stone.

He's gone to live in his home on high,
　Where hearts never ache and there's never a sigh.

The one I have loved is not dead—just gone;
　He still lives and laughs and sings his song.
He lives in the Father's house above,
　Where there's eternal happiness, peace, and love.

Such a faith will help us walk with steady step and unflinching assurance, while the shadows of sorrow hide the path from earthly view. It is faith which links us to the Father's house, as we stand silently and watch our loved ones begin their journey to the shores of eternity.

We can believe the words of Jesus, "In my Father's house are many rooms; if it were not so, would I have told you that I go to prepare a place for you? And when I go and prepare a place for you, I will come again and will take you to myself, that where I am you may be also. And you know the way where I am going" (John 14:2-4).

God would never create man and give him a restless longing for eternal life, only to deny this high aspiration He had planted in man's heart. Jonathan Swift wrote, "It is impossible that anything so natural, so necessary and so universal as death, should ever have been designed by Providence as an evil to mankind."

>The tomb is not an endless night—
>It is a thoroughfare, a way
>That closes in a soft twilight
>And opens in eternal day.

WHAT IS HEAVEN LIKE?

JESUS DIDN'T SAY very much about the environment of Heaven. Actually, that isn't very important. He did say, "In my Father's house are many rooms. . ." (John 14:2). We have all heard people talk about gold streets and diamond lights. Such speculation doesn't interest me. I am certain we can trust God, and I am sure He has adequately prepared a place of indescribable beauty. It will surpass our fondest expectations and highest aspirations. God will never disappoint us.

Many beautiful songs have been written by Fanny Crosby. She was blind and never saw the beauty of a sunset or the loveliness of a rose. She probably wrote her finest song when she dreamed about the majesty of heaven: "Some day the silver cord will break, and I no more as now shall sing; but O, the joy when I shall wake within the palace of the King! And I shall see Him face to face. . . ." Heaven will surely satisfy our deepest aspirations.

When I was a boy, my father came home one night with the news that we would be moving to another community. At first I didn't like the idea. My heart was filled with fear of the unknown. I wondered what the house and the yard would look like. I wondered if we would have close neighbors. Suddenly, it occurred to me that these things didn't really matter. Two things were foremost in my mind. First, my father would be there. The place he had chosen for his family to live would be fine. Secondly, I had complete trust in my father's wisdom and judgment. He had never disappointed me. I knew our new home would represent my father's love, and that his love had never wavered.

When I think of Heaven, I am reminded of my feelings during that boyhood crisis. Just as I knew my father would be there when we moved to a new city, I know that at death my heavenly Father will be there. Just as I recognized my father's love and concern for my well-being, I remember God's care for me and

I know that whatever provisions He has made for me will exceed my fondest dreams. To live in His presence will be joy unending.

THROUGH THE VALLEY

NOWHERE is the nature of God more perfectly described than in the Twenty-third Psalm. The essence of this beautiful hymn is contained in the first line. Say it over slowly and prayerfully; saturate your mind with it: "The Lord is my shepherd, I shall not want." The Shepherd cares for us and provides for our every need. We shall not want for strength, courage, patience, and fortitude to face life. Why? Because the Lord is always near to guide us and protect us.

Harold Bosley wrote: "Deeper than the sorrow that now engulfs us, stronger than the loneliness that will continue to tear at our heartstrings through the years ahead, more enduring than the desolation of shattered hopes and broken dreams, is the great assurance: 'Yea, though I walk through the valley of the shadow of death, I will fear no evil: for Thou art with me; .... Surely goodness and mercy shall follow me all the days of my life: and I will dwell in the house of the Lord for ever.'"

It was the custom of the shepherd to take his sheep to the highlands in order to find green pasture, and the way often led through deep gorges. When the sun was low, the valley would be dark with shadows, but the sheep were not afraid, because the shepherd was with them. They trusted him; they sensed his presence. The psalmist wrote, "Though I walk *through the valley.*" These valleys had both an entrance and an exit. And no matter how dark they were within, eventually the shepherd and his sheep would emerge into the sunshine. Death is just a dark valley through which we pass.

When Jesus knew He must die on the cross, He prayed for another way. He didn't want to die. He was only thirty-three. His heart was still full of dreams and hopes. Yet His step did not falter nor did His faith sag. He did not like the thought of suffering any more than we would, but in the Garden of Gethsemane He prayed, "... nevertheless, not my will, but thine, be done" (Luke 22:42).

Sustained by the presence of God, He walked

to Calvary, His heart full of trust in the Father. There they nailed Him to the cross. Death, to our Lord, was passing through a little dark room in the hall of life, to the living room of God. He prayed, "Father, into thy hands I commit my spirit!" (Luke 23:46).

WHAT TO DO

WHEN YOU LOSE a loved one, here are some constructive things you can do.

1. Ask God to help you. Jesus was always turning aside to spend a few moments with His Father in prayer. God will never allow life to place upon us burdens for which He does not supply the strength we need. The psalmist said, "Out of my distress I called on the Lord; the Lord answered me . . ." (Psalm 118:5). He will hear your prayer and He will guide you also—if you will place your hand in His.

I have seen the tides of tragedy sweep into many homes, often unexpectedly and without warning. Those who did not surrender to despair but were able to cope with the sudden demands of adversity without being overcome by panic were those who met God at the place of prayer.

God will never deceive us. There is within us the burning desire for immortality. Long before man had a need, God made provision for all our needs. Long before man came upon the earth, God put fertile soil and seed in the ground. Before we were born, God began storing oil, gas, and coal in the earth to keep us warm. We are subjects of His concern and creation. Jesus said, "Your Father knows what you need before you ask him" (Matthew 6:8). In order to reach the destiny for which we were created, we need immortality. God has provided that, too.

Triumph over Tragedy, a little book by Iona Henry, tells the story of her struggle for strength and courage in the face of almost overwhelming personal misfortune. First she lost her only daughter Jane to a brain tumor. Then, a major accident claimed the lives of her young son and husband, and left her seriously injured. It took a long time for the wounds of the flesh, as well as the wounds of the heart, to heal. In the dedication to her book, Mrs. Henry speaks profoundly of a timeless truth, the real source of our inspiration in time of need: "To Dad Henry, who came to meet me in the valley with God's lantern in his hand." When trouble comes, God will meet us in the dark valley. We do not walk alone.

During Jane's illness, Dad Henry wrote a letter to his daughter-in-law in which he expressed his philosophy of life. Not only was that letter of inestimable help to Iona, but it can give all of us something to keep us steady during the storms of life. Before the diagnosis of Jane's case was complete, Dad Henry wrote that he was praying that the tumor would not be malignant and fatal, but that if it was ...

"Perhaps this will help you now:

"First: Whatever happens, life must go on for you. There are too many friends and loved ones depending on you for it to be otherwise. Whatever happens to us, the stream of life must flow on. So, take good care of yourselves and don't give way to total defeat. Much in life is for you and with you, whatever comes. Keep this firmly fixed, these days.

"Second: Don't give way to 'what might have been.' We are apt to do so. We are apt to think that if we had known sooner, or if we had done differently, it would not be this way. But this is a region without boundary lines. It might not have changed results one bit. Don't linger there. You have done, and are doing, all you can in every way you know. Leave it there, for this is all any of us can do in life.

"Third: God is as sad over this as you are. It is not God's will that such things happen. Amid the many circumstances of life, some things happen because we belong to a human society. But God's will is for life to be lived to its fullness. When it isn't, He stands as of old, weeping with us.

"Fourth: We Christians believe in immortality. Whatever is commenced here will be completed There. Nothing is lost out of His care."

2. Express your grief. Don't be afraid to cry. This is nature's way to help us find relief. When Lazarus died, Jesus wept. There should be no shame in shedding genuine tears of sorrow.

But remember too that while it is good to express your sorrow, you must guard against living in a little room of self-pity. You must learn to master your grief instead of permitting your grief to control you.

3. Keep on living in a normal way. This will help the wounds to heal. When you lose someone you love, live as bravely and fully as you would if he were still present. Remember that

you are not the only one who has known such a deep hurt. Sorrow is universal. Tennyson wrote:

> Never morning wore to evening,
> But some heart did break.

Ask yourself, "How would the one I lost want me to react?" Find an honest answer to that question through prayer and meditation. In one of her poems, Edna St. Vincent Millay tells of a woman who, overwhelmed with grief after losing her husband, says, "Life must go on, I forget just why." Surely the one you have lost for a time wants and encourages you to live your whole life to the fullest.

Don't let the immediate environment of sorrow and loneliness cause you to lose your perspective. Leslie Cooke tells of a Spanish girl who was making her first visit to London. As the train made its way through the crowded and congested area of London, the girl began to weep. "These people have no view," she sobbed. Faith will help us to see, when the clouds of sorrow descend. We need not lose our view because of grief.

The more time you spend thinking about your grief, the longer it will take to heal. If you are busy helping others, you will find your own burden much easier to bear. The human mind can best focus its attention upon one thought at a time. If you do not feed your sorrow by constantly thinking about it, you will soon discover God's healing process is doing its work.

4. Develop a positive attitude. Don't think so much about what you have lost—rather, think about what you have gained. I know two women who were about the same age. Both lost their husbands about the same time. They had lived with their husbands almost thirty years. One woman refused to be reconciled to her husband's death. She lived in the past. She thought only of their yesterdays, and she ended up in a mental institution.

The other woman loved her husband just as much as the first had loved hers. She told me, just after the funeral, "I thank God for thirty wonderful and happy years with such a gentle and Christian man." She, too, had lost a great deal, but in her loss she found something for which to be grateful.

Mrs. Charles Morse was a member of the congregation I was privileged to serve in Lynn, Massachusetts. She had no children and devoted her time to her home and to helping others. For many months, she looked after her sick husband, a retired postman and artist. Through severe winters and warm summers she cared for him uncomplainingly. During the last two years of his life, she was rarely out of the house. The day after his death, Mrs. Morse and I rode together to the funeral home. We stood near the casket, and she closed her eyes and prayed, "God, I thank You for letting me live long enough and for giving me the strength to care for him until the end." What a sturdy faith —what a glorious attitude—what an unselfish spirit!

5. Remember that grief is the price we pay for the ability to love. If we did not have the capacity to love and respond to love, we would never know sorrow. The happiness I have enjoyed with those I love is greater than all the anguish I must endure somewhere down the road of life. Paul considered that "the sufferings of this present time are not worth comparing with the glory that is to be revealed to us" (Romans 8:18). Surely the joys of yesterday are more than enough to pay for the sorrows of tomorrow.

I was called to visit the parents of a young teen-age girl who had been killed in an automobile accident. "This is the blackest night we have ever faced," the father of the young girl said. "I know it is," I responded, after a long silence, "and probably the darkest night you will ever face. God didn't promise us an easy life, but He promised us all the strength we need for the journey."

She was a lovely Christian girl who had left her Christian influence on many lives. "Let me ask you a question," I remarked. "Suppose God had tapped you on the shoulder the night Susan was born, and whispered in your ear, 'I'll give her to you for sixteen years, or you can't have her at all!' What would you have said?"

"She has brought us a lot of joy," he began. "She has strengthened our faith and has brought us closer to God. To have had her sixteen years, or not to have known her at all—well, I know we would have wanted her even if it had been for only one year, five years, or sixteen years."

When we are honest with ourselves, we admit that the sorrow we know is not too high a price to pay for the joy and love we have shared with those we have lost.

6. Remember the glorious promises of God. Reassured by the comforting promises of the Bible, we can confidently face the experience of death and its unknown demands upon us.

". . . because I live, you will live also" (John 14:19).

"Shall I ransom them from the power of Sheol? Shall I redeem them from Death? O Death, where are your plagues? O Sheol, where is your destruction? . . ." (Hosea 13:14).

"He who believes in the Son has eternal life . . ." (John 3:36).

"And I give them eternal life, and they shall never perish . . ." (John 10:28).

"God is our refuge and strength, a very present help in trouble" (Psalm 46:1).

"He heals the brokenhearted, and binds up their wounds" (Psalm 147:3).

"He will wipe away every tear from their eyes, and death shall be no more, neither shall there be mourning nor crying nor pain any more, for the former things have passed away" (Revelation 21:4).

"I write this to you who believe in the name of the Son of God, that you may know that you have eternal life" (I John 5:13).

"When you pass through the waters I will be with you; and through the rivers, they shall not overwhelm you . . ." (Isaiah 43:2).

7. Commit to God the one you have lost, along with yourself. God knows how to take care of His own.

I wish I had a magic word to wipe away your tears! I do not know any magic words, but I know a God who can heal you and I commend Him to you. Remember, the door of death is the only door that leads to the Father's house. He will be waiting there to greet and welcome His children.

THERE IS A FUTURE

WHEN THE SHADOWS of sorrow settle around us, life seems to stop. We forget about the endless future, the sunrise which will never again leave those we have committed to God. For a moment, let us lift our sights from the gloom and try to catch a glimpse of the promise of our Lord, "Because I live, you will live also."

A little story from the past, almost a classic, can perhaps help us to see how to walk through the dark nights which have descended upon us.

"I was standing in front of the window of an art store in which the crucifixion of our Lord was on exhibition. Gazing intently at the display, I was hardly conscious of another person who stood alongside me. Turning around, I noticed a little boy with his eyes fixed upon the lifelike little figures in the store window.

"He was just a little mite of humanity, who stood there in ragged clothes. I thought I would see if he knew what the scene really meant. 'Son,' I asked, 'do you know Who it is?' He was quick to reply. 'Yes, sir,' he said, pointing to the Man on the center cross, 'that's our Savior.' He looked surprised that I didn't know, and with a little pity in his voice, he was eager to explain the entire scene to me.

" 'Them's the soldiers,' he continued, 'the Roman soldiers who nailed Him to the cross.' Pointing to a woman near the edge of the crowd, he said, 'That's His mother! You see! The woman who is crying.' He pushed his hands deep into his pockets as if he were waiting for me to ask other questions I wanted answered about the scene. After a long pause, he said, 'Yes, sir, they killed Him.'

" 'Where did you learn all this?' I questioned. Out of a sense of pride he gladly exclaimed, 'At the Mission Sunday School, mister.' Full of my thoughts about the good the Mission Sunday School was doing, I turned and looked at the crucifixion scene again. After a moment I slowly walked away, leaving the little street urchin still looking in the window.

"I had not walked more than a block until I heard the sound of little feet beating exultantly on the sidewalk and a childish voice crying, 'Mister! Say, mister!' Turning around, I saw the little lad running toward me. Almost out of breath, he reached my side and said, triumphantly, 'I forgot to tell you, He rose again! Yes, mister, He rose again. That's the most important part.'"

Before you let the gloom of grief settle in your heart, remember that Christ rose again. He offers us the strength and courage to face each new day with confidence. Ask for that help, and it will be yours.

Some time ago, a friend was flying me to a distant city to fulfill a speaking engagement. It was a dreary, overcast day. Just after leaving the airfield, we found ourselves climbing through clouds. At times, it was difficult to see the tip of the wings. Suddenly, ice covered the windshield and the wings were also taking on ice. The engines groaned, and although the little plane seemed to be doing its best, I was afraid it wasn't good enough. My friend reassured me that we were in no immediate danger.

"We should be breaking through the clouds,"

he said very calmly, "within the next three minutes." It was still dark, and each minute seemed like an hour. Then, it happened! We did emerge from the thick layer of clouds that had hidden the warm sunshine. Below us, like giant loads of cotton or fresh fallen snow, the clouds floated majestically along their way. Above was the morning sun and the blue sky. We could see for miles and miles. It was like getting a breath of fresh air after being in a dank and musty cellar.

This is a parable of death. Before our earthly journey is over, all of us must pass through the misty valley where our vision is obscured. We need not be afraid. Before long we will reach the other side. There the sun will break triumphantly through the clouds. The shadows of earth will be gone forever, and the vistas of a new world will be ours.

NO LAST TIME!

WHEN JESUS HUNG on the cross, He cried out in agony, "Eli, Eli, lama sabachthani?" which is interpreted, "My God, My God, why hast thou forsaken me?" (Matthew 27:46). He felt deserted, betrayed, and left alone.

Those who know the rest of the story know that Jesus was sustained in His time of desolation by the presence of God. He said later, "Father, into thy hands I commit my spirit!" You may feel alone and forsaken when the tapestry of love is torn asunder by the soft and swift feet of death, but reach out in the darkness with your lamp of faith, and God will be there to keep you.

McDonald Clarke explained death in the following beautiful statement: "Death, to a good man or woman, is like passing through a dark entry, out of one little dusty room of the Father's

House into another room that is fair and large, lightsome and glorious, and divinely entertaining."

Sir Walter Scott asked the rhetorical question, "Is death the final sleep?" He answered, "No, it is the last and final awakening."

It is difficult to get the idea of death in a manageable perspective. It is a part of God's plan for His children. Back in the 1700s Jonathan Swift, dean of Saint Patrick's, wrote, "It is impossible that anything so natural, so necessary and so universal as death should ever have been designed by Providence as an evil to mankind." It is, in fact, the only door that leads from the cramped vestibule of earthly living to the Father's House.

Henry Ward Beecher suggested, "On this side of the grave we are exiles, on the other side we are citizens; on this side, orphans; on the other side, children; on this side, captives; on the other side free; on this side disguised, unknown; on the other side, disclosed and proclaimed as sons of God."

It is never easy to be separated from those we love. It is always easier if our faith helps us to look beyond the "glass darkly" as Paul put it, to see the warm lights of the Father's House.

The following lines direct our attention to the truth of the words of Jesus when He said, "Because I live, ye shall live also."

> Do not stand at my grave and weep.
> I am not there. I do not sleep.
> I am a thousand winds that blow;
> I am the diamond glints on snow.
> I am sunlight on ripened grain.
> I am the gentle autumn's rain,
> When you awaken in the morning's hush,
> I am the swift uplifting rush
> Of quiet birds in circled flight.
> I am the soft star that shines at night.
> Do not stand at my grave and cry.
>   I am not there.
>   I did not die.

Karl Barth, considered by many to be one of the greatest theologians of this century, was once asked, "Why do so many folks come to church?" He answered, "People come to church asking the question: 'Is it true?'"

Leslie Weatherhead relates an incident in his life when he visited a friend who was caught in the grip of the dreadful disease cancer. Weatherhead says, "She was a quiet and reticent soul and it has been rather a trouble to her that, though Christ meant so much to her, she had rarely spoken of her faith to another. And then, in that room, facing the reality of a painful death she faced cancer and said, 'I am proud to be trusted with this illness. It has given me opportunities that I never had before.' " Then Dr. Weatherhead said to her, "You may not get better from cancer, but you have conquered cancer. . . ." We cannot escape death, but we can, with the help of God, conquer it.

I found this idea somewhere in my reading and may not quote it precisely, nor do I know to whom to give credit. I pass it along to you because it is a source of comfort. We often think of death as the end of something, but let us think of it as the beginning of something that never ends; we think of death of parting, but let us think of death as meeting those who have outrun us to the Father's House. We think of death as going away; let us think of it as arriving. We think of death as a final farewell; but while we are saying "farewell," there are those on the shores of eternity saying, "Good morning, forever and forever."

The late Dr. Daniel Poling had a great influence on my life. It was my privilege to visit with him on several occasions.

His young son, Clark Poling, was one of the brave young chaplains who gave his life jacket to a soldier who had no life jacket on the sinking deck of the *USS Dorchester*. Clark and the other three chaplains went down to a watery grave.

Dr. Poling said, "When Clark was a freshman in college, he came home at the end of the first semester and asked to speak with me in private. The office door was closed, and Clark looked into my face and asked this question, 'Dad, tell me for certain what you know about God.' " Dr. Poling said, "All my systems of theology left me. I had learned them so well. I said, 'Clark, I know God loves me. I know God forgives me. I know God has prepared a PLACE FOR ME.' "

In times of death, it is not what we speculate about God that brings comfort but what we know for certain about Him.

Several years ago I found a truth that is certainly the centerpiece of Christendom. I was told it was a German motto. It reads: "Those who love each other and who love the Lord never see each other for the last time." I believe this is true. I hope you believe it. Beyond the tears of Calvary are the triumphant songs of Easter, which are yet to be sung.

INSPIRATIONAL POEMS

From THERE IS NO DEATH

There is no death! The stars go down
   To rise upon some other shore;
And bright in heaven's jeweled crown
   They shine forevermore.

. . . .

And ever near us, though unseen,
   The dear immortal spirits tread;
For all the boundless universe
   Is life—there are no dead.

—J. L. McCreery

RESIGNED

From my garden of grief, with eyes that are dim,
With the raining of sorrow, *I look unto Him
Who pities and comforts,* and never departs,
Nor closes His ear to the woe of all hearts.

And out of the silence there tenderly falls
The sound of His voice as He lovingly calls.
"This is my will," it says, "mine, suffering one,"
And my heart tries to answer: "Lord, Thy will
                                      be done."

And lo! in the gloom of the heart-breaking night
There shines the bright glory of Calvary's light;
And there by her casket, so holy and fair,
It gleams like a star in the night of despair.

In the bliss of this moment of rapture I sing:
"O death, cruel monster, where is thy dread
                                      sting?"

Then chastened and calm, and with reverent tread,
I leave her with God—my dear, beautiful dead.

—Dorothy Dix Porges

Beyond this vale of tears,
  There is a life above,
Unmeasured by the flight of years;
  And all that life is love.

—James Montgomery

SHED NOT TOO MANY TEARS

Shed not too many tears when I shall leave;
   Be brave enough to smile.
It will not shorten, howsoe'er you grieve,
   Your loneliness the while.
I would not have you sorrowful and sad,
   But joyfully recall
The glorious companionship we've had,
   And thank God for it all.
Don't let your face grow tear-streaked, pale and wan:
   Have heart for mirth and song—
Rejoice, though for a little while I've gone,
   That I was here so long.
For if I thought your faith would fail you so,
   And leave you so distressed,
That sobbing to my body's grave you'd go,
   My spirit could not rest.

—Author Unknown

FOR THOU ART WITH ME

I know not when I go, nor where,
   From this familiar scene;
But He is Here and He is There
   And all the way between;
And, when I pass from all I know
   To that dim, vast unknown,
Though late I stay, or soon I go,
   I shall not go alone.

—Annie Johnson Flint

VESPERS

I know the night is drawing near,
    The mists lie low on hill and bay,
The autumn sheaves are dewless, dry.
    But I have had the day.

Yes, I have had, dear Lord, the day.
    When at Thy call I have the night,
Brief be the twilight as I pass
    From light to dark, from dark to light.

—Silas Weir Mitchell

'TIS LIFE BEYOND

I watched a sail until it dropped from sight
Over the rounding sea—a gleam of light,
A last, far-flashed farewell, and, like a thought
Slipt out of mind, it vanished and was not.

Yet, to the helmsman standing at the wheel,
Broad seas still swept beneath the gliding keel;
Disaster? Change? He left no slightest sign,
Nor dreamed he of that dim horizon line.

So may it be, perchance, when down the tide
Our dear ones vanish. Peacefully they glide
On level seas, nor mark the unknown bound.
We call it death—to them 'tis life beyond.

—AUTHOR UNKNOWN

FAITH AND SIGHT

So I go on not knowing,
   —I would not, if I might—
I would rather walk in the dark with God
   Than go alone in the light.
I would rather walk with Him by faith
   Than walk alone by sight.

—Mary Gardner Brainard

TRUST

Up the road of life I run,
Thanking God for rain and sun;
I'm not afraid of life, you see—
God's Love and Grace encompass me.

—Robert V. Ozment

From *THE LOOM OF TIME*

Not till each loom is silent
   And the shuttles cease to fly,
Shall God reveal the pattern
   And explain the reason why

The dark threads were as needful
   In the weaver's skillful hand,
As the threads of gold and silver
   For the pattern which He planned.

—AUTHOR UNKNOWN

SOMETIME WE'LL UNDERSTAND

Not now, but in the coming years,
    It may be in the Better Land,
We'll read the meaning of our tears,
    And there, sometime, we'll understand.

We'll catch the broken threads again,
    And finish what we here began;
Heav'n will the mysteries explain,
    And then, ah then, we'll understand.

We'll know why clouds instead of sun
    Were over many a cherished plan;
Why song has ceased, when scarce begun;
    'Tis there, sometime, we'll understand.

Why what we long for most of all
    Eludes so oft our eager hand;
Why hopes are crushed and castles fall,
    Up there, sometime, we'll understand.

God knows the way, He holds the key,
    He guides us with unerring Hand;
Sometime with tearless eyes we'll see;
    Yes, there, up there, we'll understand.

Then trust in God through all thy days;
    Fear not, for He doth hold thy hand;
Though dark thy way, still sing and praise,
    Sometime, sometime, we'll understand.

—Maxwell N. Cornelius

COMPENSATION

There is no loss, however great the seeming;
   There is no power to keep the soul from gain;
For life and love, however dim the dreaming
   Must end sometime in peace, all free from pain.

We love, and lose the heart's most cherished treasure,
   And life seems empty as a gaping tomb—
We feel that Grief has overfilled her measure...
   The threads of grey run thickly through Life's loom.

But underneath the heartbreak of all being
   There is the law, the Universal Call—
"Life leads to love, and love to endless giving"...
   We find our own and hold it all in all.

Each life must sometime know this great un-
veiling;
Must sometime gather up the harvest sown—
Roses will bloom through seasons never
failing . . .
The heart rejoice and grief be overthrown.

—Author Unknown

The Lights are out
   In the mansion of clay;
The curtains are drawn,
   For the dweller's away;
He silently slipped
   O'er the threshold by night,
To make his abode
   In the City of Light.

—Author Unknown

From *THE ETERNAL GOODNESS*

I know not what the future hath
   Of marvel or surprise,
Assured alone that life and death
   His mercy underlies.

. . . .

And so beside the Silent Sea
   I wait the muffled oar;
No harm from Him can come to me
   On ocean or on shore.

—JOHN GREENLEAF WHITTIER

PLEASURE AND SORROW

I walked a mile with Pleasure,
   She chattered all the way,
But left me none the wiser
   For all she had to say.

I walked a mile with Sorrow,
   And ne'er a word said she;
But, oh, the things I learned from her
   When Sorrow walked with me!

—ROBERT BROWNING HAMILTON

From LAST LINES

Though earth and man were gone,
And suns and universes ceased to be,
  And Thou were left alone,
Every existence would exist in Thee.

There is not room for Death,
Nor atom that his might could render void:
  Thou—THOU art Being and Breath,
And what Thou art may never be destroyed.

—Emily Bronte

SHOULD YOU GO FIRST

Should you go first and I remain
   To walk the road alone,
I'll live in memories' garden, dear,
   With happy days we've known.
In Spring I'll wait for roses red
   When fades the lilac's blue,
In early Fall when leaves turn brown
   I'll catch a glimpse of you.

Should you go first and I remain
   For battles to be fought,
Each thing you've touched along the way
   Will be a hallowed spot.
I'll hear your voice, I'll see your smile
   Though blindly I may grope,
The memory of your helping hand
   Will buoy me on with hope.

Should you go first and I remain
    To finish with the scroll,
No length'ning shadows shall creep in
    To make this life seem dull.
We've known so much of happiness,
    We've had our cup of joy,
And memory is one gift of God
    That death cannot destroy.

Should you go first and I remain,
    One thing I'd have you do ...
Walk slowly down that long lone path,
    For soon I'll follow you.
I'll want to know each step you take
    That I may walk the same,
For someday, down that lonely road ...
    You'll hear me call your name.

                    —ALBERT ROWSWELL

From *THE OLD ASTRONOMER*

Though my soul may set in darkness, it will
    rise in perfect light,
I have loved the stars too fondly to be fearful
    of the night.

—Sarah Williams

Death stands above me, whispering low
    I know not what into my ear:
Of his strange language all I know
    Is, there is not a word of fear.

—Walter Savage Landor

COMFORTING SCRIPTURE

The eternal God is your dwelling place,
    and underneath are the everlasting arms.

                                    DEUTERONOMY 33:27a

Wait for the Lord;
    be strong, and let your heart take courage;
    yea, wait for the Lord!

                                          PSALM 27:14

For his anger is but for a moment,
    and his favor is for a lifetime.
Weeping may tarry for the night,
    but joy comes with the morning.

                                          PSALM 30:5

God is our refuge and strength,
    a very present help in trouble.
Therefore we will not fear though the earth
    should change,
    though the mountains shake in the heart
    of the sea;
though its waters roar and foam,
    though the mountains tremble with its tumult.

Selah

There is a river whose streams make glad the
    city of God,
    the holy habitation of the Most High.
God is in the midst of her, she shall not be
    moved;
    God will help her right early.
The nations rage, the kingdoms totter;
    he utters his voice, the earth melts.
The Lord of hosts is with us;
    the God of Jacob is our refuge.

Selah

Come, behold the works of the Lord,
>how he has wrought desolations in the earth.
He makes wars cease to the end of the earth;
>he breaks the bow, and shatters the spear,
>he burns the chariots with fire!
"Be still, and know that I am God.
>I am exalted among the nations,
>I am exalted in the earth!"
The Lord of hosts is with us;
>the God of Jacob is our refuge.

>*Selah*
>
>PSALM 46

Cast your burden on the Lord
>and he will sustain you;
he will never permit
>the righteous to be moved.

>PSALM 55:22

Trust in him at all times, O people;
  pour out your heart before him;
God is a refuge for us.   *Selah*

PSALM 62:8

For he will give his angels charge of you
  to guard you in all your ways.

PSALM 91:11

When he calls to me, I will answer him;
  I will be with him in trouble,
  I will rescue him and honor him.

PSALM 91:15

Even there thy hand shall lead me,
    and thy right hand shall hold me.

PSALM 139:10

He heals the brokenhearted,
    and binds up their wounds.

PSALM 147:3

Thou dost keep him in perfect peace,
    whose mind is stayed on thee,
    because he trusts in thee.

ISAIAH 26:3

But now thus says the Lord, ...
"When you pass through the waters I will be
    with you;
    and through the rivers, they shall not overwhelm you;
    when you walk through fire you shall not be
        burned,
    and the flame shall not consume you."

ISAIAH 43:1,2

He was despised and rejected by men;
    A man of sorrows, and acquainted with grief;

. . . .

Surely he has borne our griefs
    and carried our sorrows;
yet we esteemed him stricken,
    smitten by God, and afflicted.

ISAIAH 53:3,4

"For they cannot die any more because they are equal to angels and are sons of God, being sons of the resurrection."

LUKE 20:36

I consider that the sufferings of this present time are not worth comparing with the glory that is to be revealed to us.

ROMANS 8:18

Who shall separate us from the love of Christ? Shall tribulation, or distress, or persecution, or famine, or nakedness, or peril, or sword? As it is written,
> "For thy sake we are being killed
>   all the day long;
> we are regarded as sheep to be
>   slaughtered."

No, in all these things we are more than conquerors through him who loved us. For I am sure that neither death, nor life, nor angels, nor principalities, nor things present, nor things to come, nor powers, nor height, nor depth, nor anything else in all creation, will be able to separate us from the love of God in Christ Jesus our Lord.

ROMANS 8:35-39

For now we see in a mirror dimly, but then face to face. Now I know in part; then I shall understand fully, even as I have been fully understood.

I Corinthians 13:12

For we know that if the earthly tent we live in is destroyed, we have a building from God, a house not made with hands, eternal in the heavens.

II Corinthians 5:1

... For he has said, "I will never fail you nor forsake you." Hence we can confidently say,
 "The Lord is my helper,
 I will not be afraid;
 what can man do to me?"

Hebrews 13:5b,6

Then I saw a new heaven and a new earth; . . . and I heard a great voice from the throne saying, "Behold, the dwelling of God is with men. . . . he will wipe away every tear from their eyes, and death shall be no more, neither shall there be mourning nor crying nor pain any more, for the former things have passed away."

REVELATION 21:1,3,4

PRAYER

The way is dark, O Lord; grant unto me a light of faith.
The road is steep, O Lord; help me feel the gentle touch of Your Hand.
The load is heavy, O Lord; give me the strength I need.
My heart is crushed, O Lord; place Your Hand of healing upon it.
Give me eyes to see beyond the shadows of Calvary,
And help me catch a glimpse of the glowing lights of the Father's house.
Keep me from hearing only the music of despair, O Lord,
And enable me to hear the triumphant songs of Easter . . .
I pray in the Name of Jesus Christ, my Lord and Saviour. *Amen.*